"In *Brief Black Candles* Lydia Valentine writes, 'I keep my ghosts close to know who I am.' Sounded in this note, grief and hope, life and death, dark and light—are each dispelled from their assigned binaries and winged, line by line, towards the more nuanced, more dissonant texture of a deeply human, intimately witnessed way of being in our world. This debut collection, written in the most truthful key available to language, uses poetic form and precise repetition to give shape, then echo, to questions of family, loss, justice and survival, seated in the frame of an America that is a long way from post-racial—the America of today. Valentine writes, 'It was sundown all morning. / It was raining / and it was going to rain.' In this work, we are not spared from bitter truth, nor from stubborn hope; we are given pain with love, love with pain. We are offered the heartwork of a poet committed, deeply, to 'tomorrow, and tomorrow/ and tomorrow.'"

-Sanam Sheriff

"In her debut collection, Lydia Valentine interrogates and remembers. 'I keep my ghosts close,' she writes, 'to know who I am.' And she knows who she is. With *Brief Black Candles*, Valentine names what, and who, must be named. It is her poet's work to do so. She witnesses, from within her own body, the work of survival and visibility, of accounting for all children and answering for each violence. Valentine explores the ways we touch one another and the spaces between us. 'The barrier between/ us was built by your hands.' She speaks the harms we have done; she calls us to the work of repair. 'I can't/Reasonably understand why everyone/Isn't running through the streets, screaming.' Here you will find wounds and loss. Candles extinguished, burning and drowning. Young men turned into symbols. But you will also find new and bursting life, 'stronger than any sea, any fear.' You will discover the 'swollen berry promise' of love, you will be reminded of wisdom earned in pain, 'unless it's hurting, I don't remember what to avoid.'"

-Tina Ontiveros, author of *rough house*

BRIEF BLACK CANDLES

POEMS BY

Lydia K. Valentine

Lydia K. Valentine's work

can also be found in:

*Angels Flight * literary west, aflwmag.com*
"UnNamed"

The Pitkin Review
"Bearing Witness," "Shot After Shot"

Speak, speakthemag.com
"Speaking in Tongues"

Shout! An Anthology of Resistance Poetry & Short Fiction
"Thirteen Ways of Looking at a Black Bird"

BRIEF BLACK CANDLES

POEMS BY

Lydia K. Valentine

Dedicated to the two loves of my life:

Kaia Lorraine
and
Matthew Michael

"... the miracle on which one's unsteady attention is focused is always the same, however it may be stated, or however it may remain unstated. It is the miracle of love... Some deep and ineradicable instinct... causes us to know that it is only this passionate achievement which can outlast death, which can cause life to spring from death."
- James Baldwin

"...Out, out, brief candle!
Life's but a walking shadow, a poor player,
That struts and frets his hour upon the stage,
And then is heard no more. It is a tale
Told by an idiot, full of sound and fury,
Signifying nothing."
-William Shakespeare
Macbeth, Act V, Scene 5

***

"Mom, I'm going to college."
-Amadou Diallo

"..."
-Atatiana Jefferson

"Oh my God! Why did you do that?"
-Botham Jean

"..."
-Breonna Taylor

"I can't breathe."
-Freddie Gray

"I can't breathe."
-George Floyd

"It's not real."
-John Crawford

"Why did they shoot me?"
-Kendrec McDade

"Please don't let me die."
-Kimani Gray

"I don't have a gun. Stop shooting."
-Michael Brown

"..."
-Mya Hall

"You promised you wouldn't kill me."
-Natasha McKenna

"I wasn't reaching for it."
-Philando Castile

"How did switching lanes with no signal
turn into all of this?"
-Sandra Bland

"I love you."
-Sean Bell

"..."
-Tamir Rice

"What are you following me for?"
-Trayvon Martin

THESE WORDS
AND THESE LIVES
SIGNIFY
EVERYTHING.

CONTENTS

WE ARE THE CAVALRY

It's the sound,
the slick hard sound
the burrowing scrape

of not having
not being
not doing
enough

that does it.

What's next is not
an implosion,
a swallowing down
to muffle itself
and me.

It's the bulleting crystals
of dark sprinkled screeches
that ripple and rip

a sharp burning burst
that finally eats
through to find
enough.

Let's begin.

THIRTEEN WAYS OF LOOKING AT A BLACK BIRD

after Wallace Stevens

I
Among a crowd of jeering vultures,
the only still thing
was the grace of the Black bird.

II
I was of three minds,
like a tree where
three broken Black birds swing.

III
The Black bird whirled in the blast's wind.
It is a main part of the national pantomime.

IV
A Sister and a Brother
are one.
A Sister and a Brother and a Black bird
are one.

V
I do not know which to prefer,
the beauty of our shade
or the beauty of our subtlety,
the Black bird brewing tea
or just sipping?

VI

History fills the long window
with glassed privilege.
The shadow of the Black bird
passes it, back and forth.
Denial etches
into the Shadow
a hidden rage.

VII

O haughty vessels of Babel,
why do you cling to lacquered binaries?
Do you not see how the Black birds
fly above you, reflecting every
hued letter of the rainbow?

VIII

I know towering ivory dialect
and corset-tight diction;
but I know, too,
that Black bird patois
is at the heart of all I know.

IX

After the Black bird fell,
chalk marked the edges
of one more outline.

X

At the sight of Black birds
kneeling in flashing lights,
even the mothers of strangers
should cry out sharply.

XI

He walked from 7-11
in a herald's cowl.
Bullets, not fear, pierced him
when another mistook
the purpose of his equipage:
slaying Black birds.

XII

The river is moving.
A Black bird must be dying.

XIII

It was sundown all morning.
It was raining,
and it was going to rain.
The Black bird nested
in the cedar box.

BRIEF BLACK CANDLES

Their still hearts radiate
furious sound and screaming fury

signifying everything.

Yet silence skims the surface
of their hollow homes,
their cocoons of emptiness.

Vestigial tendrils of pain
reach – growing and pulling
on those of us
left behind

yesterday, and today,
and tomorrow, and tomorrow,
and tomorrow.

A SPADE IN WINTER

"I woke up this morning/ exhausted from hiding/ the me of me.."- from *Bronx Masquerade* by Nikki Grimes

"You know, we *really*
wouldn't have had a problem
with the book,
if it had been about
good Black people...

          ...

            ...

                       Like you!"

"What did you say back?"
is the dumbfounded question
people ask
when I tell this story.
But, truth be told
      I was
           just that -

Dumbfounded. Struck dumb.
Mute. Deaf. Blind. Impaired. Helpless.
Exhausted.
Buried in hue-man soil
that gave me no
      air, no
          answer.

I could not give voice
to questions that rush to mind
years later.
What exactly is a
good Black person?
Who says
I'm one?

Is it my rape-colored skin
that makes me acceptable -
conjuring
images of House Slaves
bowing, scraping,
fetching
dinner?

Perhaps the golden
nugget that renders me wheat
and not chaff
takes the form of my White
husband,
lord and
keeper?

Does my teacher mask
(decorated with stars of
good diction,
Johns Hopkins diploma,
and sharp wit) hide
the me
of me,

thereby making me
good because you can almost
see me as
one of you - if only
I would straighten
        my hair
                a bit?

Your racist rationale
was imparted carefully,
so slowly,
to make sure that my brain,
inferior
        as it
                must be,

had a chance to grasp
your justification
of bigotry
from both you and your child
toward my Brothers,
                Sisters,
                        Children.

My stillborn response
yearns like a spade in winter,
powerful
though tarnished with the rust
of my silence,
        waiting
                to gouge.

FREEDOM COMES WITH A PRICE

Why are you screaming?

Light peers into the depths
of your throat. Yesterday's clenched
teeth no longer bar the way.
You asked to be left alone.
Perhaps the silence was not enough.

Why are you screaming?

Others have more pain
more reason more
purpose more right.
You battle against the confines
of excess while straining to swallow more.

Why are you screaming?

Surely a politely worded request
would do. A whimper can cut
as deeply as a howl and frankly
this noise is really quite enough
so now we will place the pillow

here.

MAMA

As if the sound means forever,
I hold her name humming on my lips

like desperate spasms of hope
in newly pinned butterflies.

There's weight to it-
that name she lived

for us.
She carried it

where hope writhed the hardest:
in her womb, her breast.

Tethered and unacknowledged
in that space of expected sacrifices -

> *Kids don't know a damned thing*
> *about the wounds they make and leave*
> *when they no longer make us their homes.*
>
> *They don't see the residue of our insides*
> *coating their outsides, painting them as*
> *our lost appendages.*
>
> *They don't understand that in some ways,*
> *sly cancer-coils that burrow and bide*
> *are gentler than phantom pains of loss.*

hope atrophies, calcifying
even the lightest wing,

shriveling the most obstinate
strength, until forever
is nothing but powdered grief;
ashes on my tongue.

UNNAMED

I keep my ghosts close to know who I am.
Wrapped in their silken shrouds,
I'm insulated from your ripe expectations,
from the hopeful allure of life.

Wrapped in their silken shrouds
is where my name hides
from the hopeful lure of life.
No; I can't be spoken into being.

Is *where* my name hides
your concern? It doesn't fit in your mouth.
No. I can't be spoken into being.
I'm the wrong shape, out of context.

Your concern? It doesn't fit. In your mouth,
the truth is my erasure. It began with their end.
I'm the wrong shape, out of context.
Daughter will not translate to *orphan*.

The truth is: my erasure? It began with their end.
You think you can see, hear, touch me?
Daughter will not translate to *orphan*,
so I have no meaning in this tongue.

You think you can see. Here, touch me.
I'm insulated from your ripe expectations,
so I have no meaning in this tongue.
I keep my ghosts close to know who I am.

MIDNIGHT REPAST

The heart of the Burmese
python increases in size up
to forty percent after it feeds.

I don't mean that it swells
like the diseased thing
that robbed me of my father.

No. This phenomena
is much more delicate
more sensible than that.

The heart of this magnificent huntress
creates new, healthy tissue in proportion
to the substance of her prey.

Can you imagine?

When I take you inside
my heart shrivels down,
pecking like a pebble
behind my navel.

HOLDING ON

You've placed the new dishes on the table
already. Sentries of holly wait, perched
along the freshly ironed neutral zone
of the runner, our only spectators.
There's no way to know which version of you
will appear from one dinner to the next,
no way to know what shape this meal will take
in tomorrow's reflection. There's just your
back facing me, the sound of your humming
floating – sweetness masking pungent discord
the same way the sharp bite of the ginger
floating in the soup you stir is hidden
by honey's gentle brightness. I sit down
and say nothing. You carry our stew pot
across to the table, fingers clenching
the insufficient ledge of the handles,
shifting slightly away when I reach out.

AS I LEAVE

The wind's sigh against
my rain-damp neck should
chill. Instead, heat licks
up, out, down, and down.
The sense-memory of your
breath trailing along my
tongue-wet skin echoes.

DAWN

Light flickers from the doorway,
cutting through the cottony pull of sleep
that clouds the room. A guilty fog.

You slipped away in silence,
untangling our limbs with the prolonged
carefulness of a soldier in a minefield,

and I let you think I was asleep,
allowing the obligation of words
to slide away as easily as the others.

Through the crack in the door, I watch
you shave off the prickled growth
that goes unchecked when we're together,

erasing the week from your face,
each scrape a prayer for absolution,
beads of blood welling in a nick of atonement.

I catch your eyes in the mirror,
but you blink me away.

Do you think of her
as you wash the smell of me
from your hands?

THE EPICENTER

my heart quakes with each spasm
pain radiates from my deep space

the dust of hope
clouds my mind

it obscures the innate knowledge
trembling through my body

as we wait

your hand slides into mine;
the cracks in your skin
feel like the fissures
spreading through my heart

as we watch

the dark dot looms on the screen
like a cold moon waiting to crush the planet

the doctor's words become too small
they bounce away in this new gravity

distorted sounds rattle my shell
to shake loose any remaining specks of dust

as I break

your grip squeezes so tight,
but your palm cannot press life
back into that tiny dot,

our baby's still and silent heart.

KAIA, AGE 9, SURFING

Trying again,
you get back up on the board
- laughing -
as the wave settles to silence.

You get back up on the board,
never giving up.
As the wave settles to silence,
your fearlessness steals my breath.

You never give up.
Like numbered yesterdays and tomorrows,
your fearlessness steals my breath
as you move to a place I cannot go.

Like numbered yesterdays and tomorrows-
I watch from a distance
as you move to a place I cannot go.
You – my daughter – fly free.

I watch from a distance,
laughing along as you,
my daughter, fly free,
and try again.

BEARING WITNESS

You were a promise of fierce being-ness
even as a small, silent sentinel waiting,
an island of resolve in an unreliable sea.
Circumstance never dictated your certainty,
but I didn't know if you would stay or
drown and wash away in clotted currents.

Fear, like other muscles (optimism,
triceps), requires attention and use
to increase in strength. After one loss,
it had overpowered the organic
authority of my heart and brain.

Yet, you held truth before you bore flesh,
wisdom before teeth, knowledge before
bones and breath. You, my son, a gospel
stronger than any sea, any fear,
you *are*.

SHOT AFTER SHOT:
A Sestina of Shattered Lives

I.
We had barely gotten back to our lives.
The reaper remained shrouded in shadow,
waiting in the corner. He knew enough
about this world to prepare for the shot
before it came, before tender petals
of our fragrant, fragile hope blew apart

Again. He watches the news wrench apart
the web-thin strands of peace piecing our lives
together. The sky is pregnant with ash petals.
Again, we're forced to breathe in death's shadow.
We're forced to mourn for another lost shot.
Why is this blanket of grief not enough?

We're smothering. Surely, this is enough.
No. Now, the reaping is a daily part
of our lives. The hours bleed. Another shot.
Broken pleas, the soundtrack of stolen lives,
play on. The key is the pitch of shadows.
The specter sits, smelling of burnt petals.

II.

Will reducing this union to ashes
be required to make them say, "Enough"?
Can they not see the poisonous shadow
systematically bursting us apart?
The reality is, their whitewashed lives
remain untouched by each murderous shot.

The news is full of "justified" potshots.
Fanned flames burn compassion down to ashes.
Are we so removed from each other's lives
that fellow human beings aren't enough
to fight for? Are we too blind, too apart
to see we're threatened by the same shadow?

I feel like I'm no more than a shadow
vibrating from the echoes of each shot,
watching those who look away, stay apart,
have shields from the stinging rain of ashes.
How do I tell my children they're enough
of a threat that someone could end their lives?

The reaper gently wipes away ash petals covering the
body like a shadow.
They are not enough to soak up all of the life spilled from
each unwarranted shot.
The fragments of hope float away in a blood river
sustained by lives torn apart.

FORGED TRANSITIONS

Don't Call Me Naomi...

crumbled remnants

of belief rain down

They are dead.

confused gray defeat settles

in mounds of treacherous salvation

Call Me Mara.

You have forsaken me. I renounce happiness
in every form. This flesh shall no longer be open to
your offerings. Only the burn of vinegar will fill me,
this voided vessel. Know me as Bitterness

in every form. This flesh shall no longer be open to
grace. Fetid cruelties ruin the honeyed wine of
this voided vessel. Know me as Bitterness.
I refuse to be soothed by promises of divine

grace. Fetid cruelties. Ruin. The honeyed wine of
faith is naught but another corpse to be buried.
I refuse to be soothed by promises of divine
reason. There is no reason that is reason enough.

Faith is naught but another corpse to be buried.
I dream of earthen cradles. Do not tell me to accept
reason. There is no reason. That is reason enough
to make my name mar like acid on the tongue.

I dream of earthen cradles. Do not tell me to accept
your offerings. Only the burn of vinegar will fill me
and make my name mar like acid on the tongue
as I renounce you who have forsaken me.

NIGHTMARES

The Hollywood rendered abominations
created to scratch against the metal fillings
of our hearts with foil-lined fingertips,
to send electric shivers of revulsion, of simmering dread

are grey-white skin, jagged teeth, screeching
are blank eyes, skinned-over eyes, sclera black eyes
are hunched over, misshapen, contorted bodies

are all wrong.

It's the clawing uncertainty, the polar silence
that fills a mother's belly when the sepia sun
of her world steps out beneath the deceptive
brightness of this star spangled sky, the visions that

are bullet-torn skin, broken teeth, screaming
are dead eyes, forever-shuttered eyes, bruised black eyes
are doubled-over, mis-taken, broken bodies -

these are the horrors that keep us awake.

In the Land of Now

Feral beasts, all gnashing teeth and relentless hooves,
haunt us. Down paths of silver ruin or festering hope
are the only escapes. What unholy commandment
compels these creatures with bellies full of flickering
blue-red corruption?

Paths of silver ruin or festering hope are the only escapes
in this labyrinth of gentrified larceny. We have no key
to any gate. With bellies full of flickering blue-red
corruption, the beasts have free rein to pursue, plunder,
and punish.

In this labyrinth of gentrified larceny, we have no key to
any gate. Safe passages and sanctuaries are hidden in
shadows of neutrality. The beasts have free rein
to pursue, plunder, and punish. The Apathetic,
the Hateful, and the Afraid have sanctified these actions.

Safe passages and sanctuaries are hidden. In shadows of
neutrality, silent allies are as dangerous as faulty brakes
or rotted floorboards. The Apathetic, the Hateful,
the Afraid have sanctified these actions. A toxic hive-
mind sprouts from terminal patriarchy.

Silent allies are as dangerous as faulty brakes or rotted
floorboards. What unholy commandment compels these
creatures? A toxic hive-mind sprouts from terminal
patriarchy. Feral beasts, all gnashing teeth and relentless
hooves, hunt us down.

A BREATH AWAY

an entire existence lives
in the breath between
look and *kiss*

winged horses watch and wait
equally prepared to stomp and bite
or gallop and soar

riotous vines crowd
patient pathways with love's
swollen berry promise

"If I speak in tongues of mortals and angels"

The echoed clang of my keys
in the door wakes no one.
Specters from the past
never sleep. Ever.

My shadow stretches-
as desperate as a charred wick
reaching for the stream of smoke
that thoughtlessly severs their prior bond-

using the harsh illumination
intruding from the curbside
to reach out toward the wispy
figures lurking in half-forgotten

words.

COMING OUT THE OTHER SIDE

"You're not the same as you were before," he said. "You were much more... muchier... you've lost your muchness."
- The Mad Hatter, **Through the Looking-Glass**

The wind has blown sharp
for so long   that
I don't know how to breathe
without inhaling splinters
and shards, invisible as   air.
Gas - light is so sly
like UV rays.
Deadly.

My muchness has been scraped   away
one microscopic bit at a time.
Does one notice the loss of skin cells?
No, that organ automatically
replaces, repairs, and remains
whole. The heart does   not.

The wind has blown so sharp,
for so long   that
my soul has brush burn. My most
innocent nerve endings
are ever vibrating, making it
logical to question, to   blame
myself. Apologies steam
from my pores all hours of all days,
each one a greasy, momentary salve.

BARE

"What weight rests here?" she asks,
running her cocoa-butter soft,
brown hands along my shoulders,
only warm oil between the press
of her skin against mine as she gives me
the massage we never got to last night,
our first night.

The question, like the too-soon sun,
nudges me, but I don't speak,
not wanting to think
about anyone but this woman,
about any place not beneath her body,
not beneath her hands.

I wonder if my silence was the beginning
of all that squeezed its way
between us.

CAVITIES

The twice-past drilled and filled tooth
has another gaping hole. It doesn't bother me
too much, as long as I avoid sweet foods, or cold foods,
or soft foods that might seep into its crevices to wake up
the volatile, insistent nerves that twice now
have been scraped out 'for good'.

The lesson of the gnawing ache fades every time I learn
it no matter how far down to the bone it bores.

My chart says, "Deficient working memory."

Warnings or reminders neatly printed on neural
notecards to steer me clear of the literal and figurative
pot holes I fell into previously, causing mud or shit to
seep into the seat of my jeans or life,
always seem to be written in disappearing ink or code
I forget how to read.

So, it never fails that I end up biting off a curse after
biting down on something good that then feels so bad

because unless it's hurting,
I don't remember what to avoid.

My mind won't let me forget the slate-slick knot
that quivers in my gut every time I think of my
brother, though. Persistent talons scrape against
that chalkboard substance, and the screech is a
tuning fork to my distress. I cannot find him.

There is a link between tooth decay and heart

disease. I wonder if it's because people stop eating food that is good for them and rely on what doesn't make their brokenness feel bad.

I wonder if I will get the tooth pulled this time or just try to repair it.

Again.

CRASHING

Dangerous happiness slicks

the path between me and you and you and me

andmeandyouandyouandmeandmeandyouandyouandme

andmeandyouandyou-

black ice.

It holds in the colors of this jagged love

      fevered orange hunger

      bruised purple expectation

      musky yellow hope

mixed and mired into a whole mess

coated with its sheen

stretched sheer

as far as grace allows.

AFTER

The griminess of her soul seeped

through the cracks between her teeth

as if her smile were a scar on the moon

and chaos was all that could follow.

THE SKIN I'M IN

is mommy-soft, care-worn
stretches to fit the codes that switch
throughout my day

recognizes like-fabrics: not separated
by colors but grouped by ability
to tumble through life together
without too much static

feels too tight when my tag
is mis-read and I am washed
in a light meant for someone else

can only give you a clue to what's inside
my ancestral closet: skeletal hangers
of black, red, and white,
full-blood, mulatto,
octoroon, quadroon,
half-breed, mixed,
and altogether
all mixed up

has thirty-three years
of layers that have finally
learned to be thick enough
to repel disapproval
and judgments
so that they don't sink in
most of the time
or at least some
of the time
anyway

THE HANDS THAT SHAPE

my hands are - often- dry and rough
and through the cracks you can see
the legacy of my father,
whose hands built a foundation
of family as solid as the beams
he forged in J & L Steel Mill

a man's hands, doing work in a place
that saw him as the man he was and not
the Boy he'd been forced to be
in the confines of the Jim Crow South
where he learned the strength and grief
and duty of being a man, a real man

from the mother who raised him
on her own - tying on the shackles
of a maid's apron strings and cleaning
houses so that her children wouldn't
have to - and the specter of a father
who was not man enough to stay.

His work, his life, hardened his hands
but they were never too hard to gently hold
the hand of my mother

whose thin, golden fingers
provided the mold from which mine were cast
and showed me the graceful strength
that is needed to take the hand of another
to build a life and a family together
and taught me the confidence

to know that I could do anything
on my own and do it well
including shape a life for myself,
for my children, if a partner
worthy enough to take my hand
and walk beside me never came along.

ROAD STORIES

for Zhenya

I.
She says, "There are many different kinds of beauty,"
pointing at the horizon and the mist resting gently
on the hip-like curve of the Green Mountains,
telling about her Ukrainian flatlands and the sonorous
rains of Vancouver.

Her bright smile cuts through the gray morning
as we walk and a quick laugh is never too far behind,
the magnificence of her youth and her freedom
reflected in the vibrant, wild growth around us.

II.
"Why is your small child white?" The question
spills forth as brisk as the wash of mountain air.
After the analogous description of coffee with cream,
we compare our stories of family complexities.
She tells me how her father's parents objected
to the colorful, creative strains of her mother's people,
that they wouldn't allow her to call them Grandmother
and Grandfather, and refused to help with any need.
Her young parents, not yet successful, wintered
with no hat to cover her infant head.

I know the pain that her mother felt, due in part to the
rejection of her ethnic difference, but even more because
of the rejection of her child. Now that these in-laws,
elderly and penitent, are the ones who need help,

her mother must swallow the hurt that comes with saying their names and find a way to fit a cap of forgiveness over her heart.

III.
"My grandfather tosses pennies along the road as he walks," she says as we trudge up the hill. "Just for fun... This way he can point out where he has been, giving the unremarkable highway something to be remarked upon." She invites me into her world with her words, and I can see the older man walking with his big stick in one hand, jiggling coins in the other, smiling as he sends one off to meet its mate waiting in the dust.

When I return home, I will think of the dips and crests of her voice as it punctuated our walks with copper-bright observations, and wonder what stories she is collecting along the path of her travels to Germany, Beijing, Colorado, and home again to the Ukraine, marriage, and motherhood.

TESTING SUPER POWERS

When I was three, I shut my tongue
in the jamb of the bathroom door.

I vaguely remember pinching
my tongue and marveling at the utter lack of pain.
I don't know why I was squeezing
my tongue in the first place,

but I became suspicious of my pinching skills.

Maybe my fingers simply weren't strong enough.
Or *maybe* I had a super-strong tongue-
the start of my super powers!

I needed some proof before running
to tell Lynette and Lamont the big news.
And so, I set my tongue in place and pushed
the door closed with one determined swing

only to find agony in its kryptonite-grasp.

Neither my super-power dreams
nor my three-year-old arms were enough
to liberate my tongue. After an hour - or five seconds
passed with me stuck, crying and afraid of

how mad Mommy would be at this latest caper,

but more afraid of being trapped until my tongue
broke off, the Wonder Woman of 144 Fourth Avenue
swooped in to save me. There was no anger

when she freed me from the mess that I had gotten
myself into. She hugged me so tight I could feel the
breath rushing out of her flared nostrils, and the bony
point of her collarbone dug into my cheek, and she

brought me icy-sweet popsicles
to soothe my swollen tongue.

SONNET OF A MOST AUSTERE AND LONELY OFFICE

"May you have children who are just like you,"
she said smiling, with eyes as sharp as glass.
I recognized the curse when I heard it,
a blessing of malice to kick my ass.

It didn't matter; I hoped they would be.
I would be different and better than her.
No acrid, pack-a-day smoke in my house.
No wounds from cutting eyes to remember.

Laughs, loud and long, not skin prickling silence,
are what they'd know to expect or to dread.
No concert would pass with my seat unclaimed.
No tightrope to walk made only of thread.

But what did I know of a mother's pain?
Love heals, burns, chokes, and heals again. Again.

RESTLESS

I weave through cottony darkness, seeking,
seeking the fine silvery thread that will
lead me, lead me, out of this quilted state
of restlessness. Insomniatic nights
coupled with coffee-fueled days shake me,
shake my tenuous grasp on right and left,
up and down, back and forth; obscuring my
path, my place, my poem, altering
the pieces and peace of me.

TIGER ROSE

Annabelle Mingo was a whiskey-drinking,
moonshine-making lady before
Alzheimer's made her dried and splintered.

T.R., as my daddy called her,
was always trying to get somebody
to bring her some Tiger Rose.

No one would.

Mommy called her Mama, not Grand.
I don't know why, and there's no one left
to ask.

Chelle's Black Power Fist sank halfway
into the mud of Blacky's pen when
Annabelle threw it out the window.

I never saw it in Chelle's room again.

Taking her to the ER, when I was four,
I called out to Mommy, "Mama's not here anymore."
I was sitting beside her in the backseat.

I knew that she was gone but not enough
to be sad.

A KINDNESS OF CROWS

Cruel headlights live in the moments
between awake and asleep.
With the ruthlessness of a crow
- too committed to be nostalgic -
I tear apart what before
had seemed full of life.

Organ meat
supple yet firm
slippery and sweet,
useless in the misshapen carcass,
is now nourishment for anticipated flight.

THE QUIET SHAME OF WINTER

barren and bereft after
being stripped of her bounty
the memory of her fullness
of her lavish conceit

      spilling her beauty to be
      stepped on and spoiled

is all that remains inside

of her

CANYON WALLS

Time dulls the jagged edges of our lives.
Former rough-hewn boulder ledges reaching
to bridge a crevice that was always there,
to meld so completely as to conceal
the cracks, now rest alongside the canyon
walls of a marriage worn down to ruin
by the steady drip of half-truths, untruths,
and the harsher truth that time cannot heal
the wounds that you refuse to acknowledge.

THE PULL OF HOME

When I think of the home of my youth,
it is always full close to bursting:
aunt and uncles - raised like older siblings,
their friends who came and went or sometimes stayed,
the dogs, perched sentinels in the yard,
laughter, "fussin' and fightin'"- fever pitch,
not enough room - no space to have as mine,
to make out the quiet noise of my thoughts.

The ones that came before us left.
The corners filled with stories, jokes, and bickering
became mute; the walls seemed to pull in even closer
as the space between them became a suffocating
emptiness.

But when everyone is all there, together, again -
drawn back by the magnet of family,
meaning returns to the red-shingled house
and those who remain inside.

THAT SEPTEMBER

It was the mouse that pushed
me over the edge.

on our own in Philly
car struts that defied repairing
a tuition bill that didn't match
          my salary

Really, though, it was the mouse
that pushed me over the edge.

my father, dead
her father, absent
a girl-school that "didn't get" my
          "very boy-like" 4-year-old

However, I honestly tell you,
it was the mouse.

two planes ruptured
          a nation's peace
propelling xenophobic
          panic

But, damn it,
I would have been fine
had that mouse not invaded
and propaganda regarding
rodents and their deadly diseases
hadn't been thrust upon us,
launching security levels:

low-risk-green (no sighting)
to severe-risk-red (droppings all around)
leaving me trembling in the dark,
Valium and cell phone in hand.

pining

the green scent of you swims through my mind.
floating would be too common -
the fringe of sparrows' wings
moving across a monotonous sky.

you are not an average happening
but one that is lush and ripe
so that the very air changes substance
upon your presence.

Ferguson, Missouri, USA

Feeling out of sorts
Everything is too tight
Restricting my air
Grabbing my insides
Until all I think of and
See are the dreams left
On the ground
Next to him, next to

Michael Brown.
"I don't have a gun.
Stop shooting."
Since I heard about the murder
Oily streaks of anger and despair
Undulate through me, and I can't
Reasonably understand why everyone
Isn't running through the streets, screaming.

Unwillingly, this young man is left to be a
Symbol of all that we try to breathe
Around, to live through, to ignore.

REQUIEM FOR A MOTHER

At the start, a drying riverbed is not arid
but
    slick
        with muddy
            grief.

The sentiments left behind do not
crumble
    easily
        to be
            brushed
                away.

They cling to my soul in the instant
of
    each
        slurping
            step.

Molds in the shape of my loss
are
    ringed
        with reaching
            fingers.

The cracks to come will show the
consequence
        of your
           slow
              disappearance.

SCHOOL BOARD MEETING

As you begin to speak, arms spread and reaching,
ghost-like waves of hostility pearl into words
coated – at first - with a sheen of oily deference.
"I want nothing more than safety, comfort for us all."

Ghost-like waves of hostility pearl into words.
The crudeness of bigotry oozes slyly through the room.
"I want nothing more than safety, comfort for us all.
We're endangered by the trendiness of appeasing..."

The crudeness of bigotry oozes slyly through the room
leaving pestilent sludge in the wake of your comments.
"We're endangered by the trendiness of appeasing
radical minority groups who see illusion as reality."

Leaving pestilent sludge in the wake of your comments,
you shed any pretense of compassion and goodwill.
"Radical minority groups who see illusion as reality,
you are an assault on the natural order of life."

You shed any pretense of compassion and goodwill.

"I'm blessed that my kids are normal & feel sorry for you."

<u>You</u> are an assault on the natural order of life.

Those who live in love, live in God, & God lives in them.

I am blessed that my kids are normal & feel sorry for <u>you</u>.

Instead of kindness and peace, you have only fear.

Those who live in love, live in God, & God lives in them.

You can't extinguish the blazing light of their truth.

Instead of kindness and peace, you have only fear,

coated – at first - with a sheen of oily deference.

You can't extinguish the blazing light of their truth

as you speak, arms spread and reaching.

RADIATION

we are drowning
drowning in the ashes
the ashes of you

death is a wind

we are tiptoeing
tiptoeing around
your delicacy
cementing every pane
cementing every shutter
cementing oh-so-pretty
leaden drapes to the wall

you wait by the window

we are watching
watching for the breeze
the breeze we keep trying to shut   out.

SPEAKING IN TONGUES

*Dedicated to the families of Trayvon Martin, Michael Brown,
Tamir Rice, and too many others to name.*

When they come
       in this time-
       in this place-
Niemoller's Socialists aren't first.

The strange flotsam jettisoned
with guns, garbage bag nooses,
metal-lined vans, and more guns
are named

Amadou,
       and Oscar,
Trayvon,
       and Michael,
Sandra,
       and Tamir

to #SAYTHENAME of a few.

       In this time-
       In this place-

Our rage-full voices spill out in protest, but
the dam you fashion from concrete blocks of

DenialDetractionDisbeliefDisinterst
DenialDetractionDisbeliefDisinterst
DenialDetractionDisbeliefDisinterst
DenialDetractionDisbeliefDisinterst
DenialDetractionDisbeliefDisinterst
DenialDetractionDisbeliefDisinterst
DenialDetractionDisbeliefDisinterst
DenialDetractionDisbeliefDisinterst
DenialDetractionDisbeliefDisinterst
DenialDetractionDisbeliefDisinterst

stops the viscous swamp of our agony
from reaching you.

While you watch from the banks of privilege,
we wade in water as thick and ropy as clotted dreams:
    to live while black...
    to marry who we love...
    to use the bathroom...
    to keep pipelines out of ancestral lands...
    to escape land mines, genocide, and other thieves
            that steal children and grandmothers.

We wade in these systemic waters
trying to have the breath to live,
the peace to live, the freedom to - simply - live.

Our light bright to midnight skin warps and prunes.
The water stirs and pulses with our voices,
our steps, and pushes against your concrete impassivity.

You look away and began to consider-
blustery defensiveness stalls progress,
but you *begin* to *consider* the sandbags
you've stacked and keep on hand to
– righteously! – protect your position.

But now,

> in this time-
> in this place-

Now the shore deteriorates beneath you,
you who stood so certain, so safe before.

Now you reach out your hand, hoping
to share in our buoyant resilience.

Now you speak out in confusion and fear,
beginning to imagine the torment
of drowning by degrees in the sputum
of ruptured justice.

You.

You remind- no, scold! - us
that *movements are stronger*
when we come together
even though the barrier between
us was built by your hands,

and we are asked- no, admonished! -
to disregard that dam and the damning
consequences of your past silence,
even though the raw-meat smell
of our children's blood clings to both.

Forgive and forget slithers smoothly
from transgressors' tongues. You present
these nonsense syllables as if you're an
oracle of the divine, but your purpose,
your ploy, is far from holy. I know.

Still, I will raise my hand from the
chest-deep depths I've forcibly come to know.
I will reach across the rough concrete
of your ignorance and help you stand
in your new waterlogged reality,
in your pool that barely reaches the knee.

I dare you to call yourself a survivor.

I've been teaching myself to draw during the quarantine, and since my daughter graduated from college this May, of course I drew a picture of her in celebration.

I wanted to post the drawing from the moment it was finished, but - and this is hard even to think, let alone write - every time I look at it, I can't help but be reminded of Michael Brown, who would have turned 24 on May 20th had he not been murdered by a police officer (whose name I intentionally refuse to write) in Ferguson at 18. I can't help thinking about his mother, Lezley McSpadden, whose picture of her son in his high school cap and gown, the picture that celebrated his accomplishment and personified the promise of his future, became instead the visual elegy for her son, her baby, and his promise. I think about how last August, on the fifth anniversary of his murder, Ms. McSpadden wrote an editorial "because the continuing execution of black and brown young people by law enforcement has not stopped, or even slowed down... And because more of us must continue the drum beat toward criminal-justice reform." I'm telling y'all, I don't think that I have her strength. Actually, I know that I don't. This woman not only still lives (period), she still lives in Ferguson and ran for City Council this year in her continued fight to give voice to the unheard and to make changes for the better. Meanwhile, I feel grateful that shelter in place means that my kids are out and about less, so the ever-present bullseye of their black and brown skin is less available for target practice.

THE LOADS WE CARRY

So many people are struggling with uncertainty and fear for themselves, their loved ones, and even those in their greater community who they do not know at all or very well as the threat of COVID-19 has grown from being something affecting other countries, to something killing the elderly, to something spreading rampantly through our country, state, and the lives of people they know.

Over these recent months, the risk of being marked for death by this insidious virus has elevated stress levels significantly, and the allostatic load (the cumulative wear and tear resulting from that chronic stress) is wreaking havoc on people's day-to-day mental and physical well-being because the body and brain have continuously been biologically functioning in a heightened state of fight-flight-or-freeze. Every day. For months. While the responses that allow people to react to threats are helpful-even necessary - in brief bursts, when peril feels ever-present, when danger looms despite taking precautions or following the rules outlined by those in charge, when hazards take the form of innocuous activities of regular, daily life, those very same biological responses lead to systematic malfunction. Fatigue and forgetfulness. Difficulty focusing and reading. Insomnia, loss of appetite, and increased risk of cancer and heart disease.

It's a wonder that people have been able to accomplish much of anything under these circumstances.

Now consider living in these conditions for a year. Three. Eight... Trayvon Martin was killed eight years ago on February 26, 2012. While his was not the first murder stemming from unjust violence and systemic racism toward black people, for many Black Americans it - and the subsequent acquittal of his murderer - led to either the beginning of or the increase in the heightened state of fight-fight-or-freeze in which we live every day. We have gone to work and school, found ways to smile and chat, remained professional and productive despite the allostatic overload of peril that feels ever-present, danger that looms despite following the laws of this country, and the hazards that come from simply trying to live while Black.

ABOUT THE POET

Lydia K. Valentine is a playwright and poet, director and dramaturg, editor and educator. Her proudest accomplishment, though, is being a mom to two caring, creative, and intelligent humans. Through her own writing and the projects to which she contributes under Lyderary Ink, Lydia seeks to amplify the voices of those who are often stifled, ignored, and marginalized in what has been the  accepted narrative of the United States. She is currently working on *The Virus*, a play set in the year 2095 (50 years after the eradication of COVID-19) which explores the legacy of both the pandemic and systemic racism, inequity, and injustice.

NOTES & ACKNOWLEDGEMENTS

I have deep gratitude to everyone who has helped me in any way in my life. Without Benjamin Gorman and Not a Pipe Publishing, this book would not exist. Thank you for seeking me out, believing in my work, and committing to getting it out in the world. The support that you and Zack Dye have given to me and many other diverse voices - well before it became *de rigueur*- has changed lives. Representation matters at Not a Pipe well beyond the hashtag.

Thank you to the editors of the other publications (print and digital) in which some of the poems in this collection first appeared (sometimes in earlier versions). Thank you to the brilliant writers Christine Robbins, Matthew Silva, and Kaia Valentine, for not letting our relationships get in the way of providing detailed, honest, line by line revision suggestions for this collection. Additional thanks and love to you three for all of the support, strength, laughs, and love you have given to me over the years.

Thank you to Kari Fisher for our virtual Minnesota - Washington poetry workshop that started in 2015 and has kept me writing through the many times when I otherwise would have stopped. Kari was the first reader for many of these poems, and her thoughtful feedback helped me to beat them into shape.

Thank you to Nichole Dupont for being my writing buddy and sister-friend at Bread Loaf and beyond. Keep kicking ass! *Je t'aime.*

Thank you to Cody Pherigo for always sending me encouragement and writing prompts, for sharing rejuvenating time and space, and for validating my most Pisces of moments.

Thank you to Chandra Ganguly for being an inspiration as a writer, businesswoman, and mom.

Thank you to Carolyn Hosannah, Andala Wagner, Mark & Maggie Dahl, Deana, Guillaume, Max, & Marcus Wiatr, Lisa, Dmitri, & Stella Keating, Alex Koerger, and Pam Dionne for feeding my body and soul, providing easy silence, creating the introvert/extrovert party (Lisa!), and always making me feel at home. Thank you to Emma Coopersmith for our beautifully silent writing workshops during which we typed each other feedback instead of talking, even though we were in the same room. It might seem strange to neurotypical people, but it was the best!

Thank you to Dede Johnson, Chevi Chung, Indiigo Klyne, April Lorenzo, Marilyn Bennett, Luzviminda Uzuri "Lulu" Carpenter, Richard Kalustian, and Jenise Petrich for safe space, real talk, and conversations that can be had with just a look.

Thank you to Tina Ontiveros, my sister from another mister, for making me laugh, for listening, for sharing your work, for giving and taking honest feedback, for explaining publishing and business ins and outs, and for writing The Idiot's Guide to Lydia. I am so proud of you and Rough House! I would not have made it through Goddard without you.

Thank you to all of my teachers, especially Bob Eldridge, who has been a guide, mentor, and friend to me for over 30 years, and also to Joan Cucinotta, who always makes time to answer questions on writing, teaching, and mothering. I have never-ending gratitude to Mrs. Fields, Ms. Cuffie, and Ms. Cobb, all three of whom brooked no nonsense, but made us feel seen, heard, and loved. I am indebted to the kindness, generosity of spirit, and wisdom extended to me by Pam McCauley, Caroline Spear, and LaQuasha Lewis, three extraordinarily strong women who I am honored to have had as friends

For me, everything begins and ends with family... There is no thanks deep, wide, or strong enough for my parents, Lorraine and Lamar Roberts, and my aunt Michelle Worthy, who gave me the tools to be the writer, reader, and thinker that I am, who never failed to believe in me, who truly made me think I could accomplish anything I set my mind to, and who I hope are proud of me. I wish they were here to share in this accomplishment. So very many thanks to my amazing sisters, Lynette Crumity and Laurice Roberts, who packed up to move across the country with me, who always support my grand ideas (like moving across the country), and who keep me laughing and shaking my head in our sister chat! Thank you to my brothers, Thomas Willis, Logan Roberts, and Lucien Roberts, who always take time to chat and give me a boost when I need it. Additional thanks to Lucien, who talked through many aspects of my play and writing in general with me (reminding me to "kill my darlings!"), and Laurice for late night writing sessions. Thank you to my incredible nephews Jordan, Noah, and Ethan Crumity, and to Salvatore Cindrich, all of whom nerd out with me about comics, superhero movies, sci-fi and fantasy geekery, and art. I'm looking forward to future collaborations, guys!

Additional thanks to Salvatore for the beautiful cover art that is everything I hoped it would be and more.

Thank you to Na'Ima Perkins who sees me and who helps me to see myself as the best version I can be. From Johns Hopkins to Turkey and Washington, you have been and continue to be my anchor, my most enthusiastic cheerleader, and my light. There are no words.

Finally, thank you to my babies, Kaia and Matt, for being delightful (ha!) and for making me wonder, dream, and laugh (and laugh!). Thank you for game nights and hide-and-go-seek. Thank you for believing in me and loving me. Thank you for the brightness that fills me when I see you or hear your voices and laughs. You are the two halves of my heart.

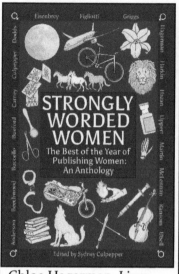

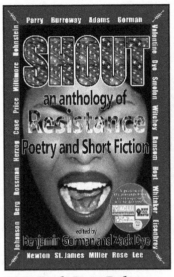

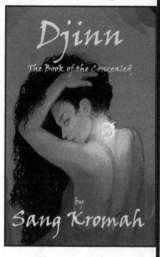

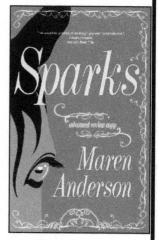